WITHDRAWN

Community Challenge Campaign
1999

Decorating
Pots

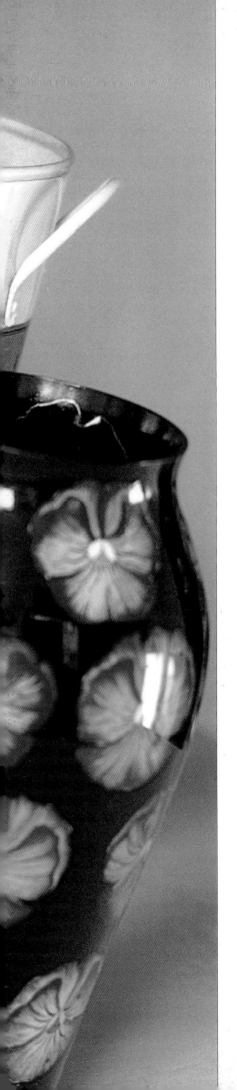

Decorating
Pots

25 creative
projects
to make

Stephanie
Donaldson

COLLINS & BROWN

First published in Great Britain in 1999
by Collins & Brown Limited
London House
Great Eastern Wharf
Parkgate Road
London SW11 4NQ

Distributed in the United States and Canada by
Sterling Publishing Co, 387 Park Avenue South,
New York, NY 10016 USA

9 8 7 6 5 4 3 2 1

British Library Cataloguing-in-Publication Data:
A catalogue record for this book
is available from the British Library.

ISBN 1 85585 663 8 (hardback edition)
ISBN 1 85585 697 2 (paperback edition)

Designer: Roger Daniels
Photography: Michelle Garrett

Reproduction by HBM Print Ltd, Singapore
Printed in Hong Kong by Midas Printing

Contents

Introduction

Why, you may ask yourself, would you want to decorate a pot, given that every gift shop and department store seems to be filled with such items? Well, there are a number of good reasons. It's fun, it's inexpensive and it allows you to be creative and get great results without needing any specialist knowledge. Whether you realize it or not, we are all creative to some extent; what we lack is not creative ability, but confidence in that ability.

Each of the projects in this book is designed to be easily achievable at home using readily available materials and a pot bought from a garden centre or high street store. No experience or special skills are needed, simply a desire to spend some time being enjoyably creative. Even if you have never done anything like this

before you will be able to achieve good results by following the simple step-by-step instructions given for each project. Once you have gained confidence, you can add your own touches, adapt or interpret, or even have a go at the alternative versions which are suggested for each idea.

The desire to embellish and decorate pots is as old as history itself. The earliest decoration had a practical purpose – simple clay domestic vessels had patterns scratched on them with twigs to identify the owner and avoid conflict with other members of the tribe. As life became more settled, those early scratchings developed into painted or relief patterns – and so the decorative arts had their beginnings. Ever since, domestic ware has been decorated according to tribal traditions or the fashions of the day, and this book is simply a continuation of that long tradition.

Although we tend to think of pots as being made from earthenware or china, the dictionary definition is 'a rounded vessel of earthenware, metal or glass for holding liquids or solids'. The projects in this book reflect this definition in that they feature many shapes and sizes of pots made from a variety of materials. Although the measurements of the pots are given in each project, remember that these are meant as guidelines and there is no need to spend time looking for a pot of exactly those dimensions. Similarly, you can allow for some variation in shape as well, although for certain projects it is recommended that you use the shape illustrated.

Nowadays, most garden centres have a huge range of terracotta pots available in every imaginable shape and size. Many are imported from the Far East and although

they are not always ideal for the garden, as they tend not to be frost-proof, they are perfect for decorating, especially if they are to be used indoors. Look out for old terracotta pots in junk shops as they have wonderful character and are ideal for projects such as the beaded or gilded pots. You can protect polished surfaces from being scratched by the terracotta by attaching felt stickers to the base of the pot.

Any department store, gift shop, or retailer which specializes in accessories for the home will have a huge range of plain vases and pots in china, glass and metal which are inexpensive to buy and can be used for these projects. When you are buying new pots you should generally look for something as plain as possible, but if it is for a project where the entire surface is to be covered you can buy something with a pattern on it. Decorated pots, which have proved unpopular with the public, can often be bought for next to nothing in the

sales and it is also worth looking in local junk shops for pots which could benefit from a make-over.

Before embarking on any of the projects in this book take time to read the instructions – this may seem boringly obvious, but it will save frustration later when you may discover that you do not have some vital ingredient. There are certain useful materials and equipment which it is worth buying to keep at hand for craft work: large and small good-quality sharp scissors, a scalpel knife, a metal ruler, tracing paper, carbon paper, PVA glue, clear craft glue, spray mount, wallpaper paste, household and artist's paintbrushes and a basic set of acrylic paints. A glue gun can also be useful but unless you are very careful it tends to leave fine filaments of glue everywhere. Store your craft materials together, preferably out of sight of children and other marauders, so that when you are feeling creative they are readily at hand rather than scattered around the house and garage. Art shops are the usual source for most of the materials needed in this book, but with the huge interest in decorative paint finishes, stencilling and so on, many of the large DIY outlets now also carry a good selection.

The projects in this book use four main types of paint – emulsion, clear varnish, acrylic and spray paint. You probably won't need to buy emulsion paint specially for a project as most of us tend to hoard quarter-full tins of emulsion paint – next time you're having a clear out, go through these tins, throwing away anything that has gone lumpy, and decanting the rest into coffee jars. It will keep just as well and you can instantly see what colours you have available. If necessary you can use the acrylic paints to deepen the colour of an emulsion paint. Many clear varnishes are now water-based and quick-drying and are ideal for these projects. A little goes a long way so you should buy the smallest tin available. Buy a basic set of acrylic paints plus burnt umber (which is used to tint varnishes), and maybe some other earth pigments such as raw ochre and burnt sienna. Water-based aerosol paints are now available in a good range of colours in matt and satin finishes especially for craft work.

If this list of materials and equipment seems rather daunting, remember that you can probably manage with much less – after all, primitive man started with nothing more than a lump of clay and a twig, and look what developed from there.

Newspaper Collage

Georges Braque often used pieces of newspaper in his collages and his pictures were the inspiration for this vase which has been covered in a collage of foreign newspapers. It isn't essential to use foreign papers but they do give the vase a cosmopolitan air and the words take on a more abstract appearance. Once the collage is complete the vase is sealed with coats of tinted satin varnish to create a durable surface.

Bring newspapers back from a holiday abroad, or check with larger newsagents who may carry foreign papers for expatriates. They will often sell out-of-date papers very cheaply.

Tools and Materials

china vase – 30cm (12in) tall

newspapers

scissors

soft paintbrushes

pva glue

wallpaper paste

burnt umber acrylic paint

water-based satin varnish

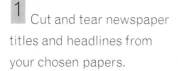 Cut and tear newspaper titles and headlines from your chosen papers.

2 To seal the newsprint, paint the pieces of newspaper with a mixture of 1 part PVA glue to 2 parts water and allow to dry.

3 Brush the wallpaper paste onto the reverse of each piece of paper and onto the vase and then position the papers, smoothing any creases and overlapping as you go to ensure that the entire vase is covered. Leave to dry.

Comic Book Collage

Use comics for a children's version of this vase. Actually, comics look so good when used for collage that you may find that you want to keep it for yourself.

4 Mix a very small amount of burnt umber acrylic paint into the satin varnish to tint it and then paint it onto the vase. Be sure to pay párticular attention to the rim and the base where a good seal is essential. Allow to dry and then apply at least two further coats. For a really smooth finish you can add several more coats, but this is not essential.

The Midas Touch

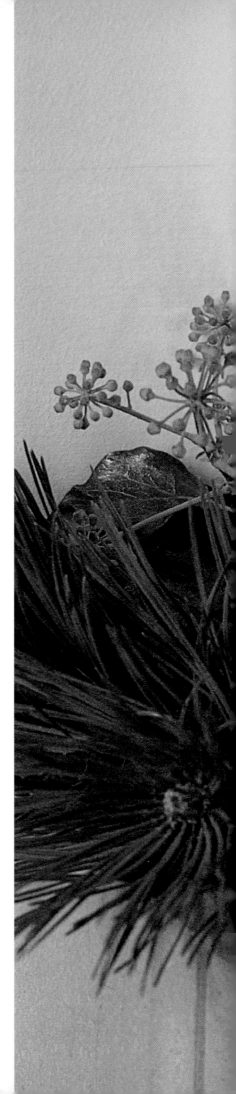

Add glowing light to the Christmas mantelpiece with gilded terracotta pots containing night lights. By gilding the pots inside as well as out, the candlelight is enhanced and the festive theme is given a simple but stylish emphasis. These pots also look wonderful when used to light the dinner table.

Dutch metal, a less expensive and easier-to-use alternative to real gold leaf has been used for these pots. The metal leaf is sold in sheets mounted on wax paper and is applied to a surface that has first been painted with 'size' which sticks the metal leaf to the pot. Once you have discovered how easy it is to transform humble objects into gilded treasures you will have to restrain yourself from gilding everything in sight.

Tools and Materials

**old terracotta pots –
10cm (4in) diameter –
thoroughly cleaned**

paintbrush

**gold size
(available from art
shops or specialist
paint suppliers)**

**dutch metal leaf
(as above)**

scissors

very soft brush

a soft cloth

1 Paint size onto half of the pot interior and leave to dry for 5 minutes.

2 Cut sufficient angled strips of metal leaf to cover the inside and outside of the pot, then carefully lay strips of Dutch metal onto the sized surface with the metal leaf in contact with the size. Press into position.

3 When the whole of the sized area is covered with strips of metal leaf, gently lift away the wax paper.

4 Very gently brush the leaf with the soft brush. This will lift away any excess leaf and smooth the leaf into any irregularities on the surface.

Pewter Pot

Dutch metal is also available in silver, pewter and bronze, all of which can be used in the same way.

5 Repeat this process for the other half of the pot interior and then the exterior.

6 Leave to fix for 2 hours then rub over with the soft cloth to burnish and remove any loose metal leaf.

Sponged Mosaic

Painted decoration need be neither intricate nor time-consuming to be effective, as this very easy sponged decoration demonstrates. Like the best folk art it uses readily available materials and simple techniques to achieve its effects.

Three colours of acrylic paint have been slightly thinned down with water and then applied to the pot using ordinary household sponge cut into small squares. The pattern is deliberately random as this works better than a repeat pattern would on the uneven surface of this irregularly shaped pot. Repeat patterns require greater precision as well as a symmetrically shaped pot to be successful.

Tools and Materials

**terracotta wall pot –
18cm (7in) tall**

**sponge-backed
scouring pad**

scalpel knife

scissors

acrylic paints

paintbrushes

paper towel

clear satin varnish

1 Cut squares from the scouring pad using the scalpel knife to cut through the sponge for a clean cut.

2 Use scissors to cut through the coarse backing.

3 Mix the acrylic colours with water in a 50/50 mix.

Diamond-patterned Pot

Paint the pot with a solid colour and then use different sized sponges to apply a diamond pattern in a contrasting colour.

4 Dip the sponges in the paint, removing excess paint when necessary by pressing the sponge onto a paper towel and then press the paint-loaded square onto the pot to create the pattern. When complete, leave to dry.

5 To seal the design, paint the pot with clear satin varnish. Leave to dry.

Black Magic

Découpage on glass is not as well known as the more usual examples of this craft which is a pity as it can be quite stunning. It was very popular in Victorian times when ladies whiled away the hours creating intricate designs of great complexity. The effect is achieved by sticking the images to the inside of the glass and then painting the inner surface to give the finished object a wonderful depth and background.

This modern interpretation of an old craft is far less intricate and time-consuming. A clear glass vase has been transformed with nothing more than cut-outs from a sheet of wrapping paper and a can of black aerosol enamel paint.

Tools and Materials

wide-necked glass vase – 25cm (10in) tall

sheet of wrapping paper with clearly defined images

pva glue

paintbrush

wallpaper paste

plastic bag

adhesive tape

black enamel aerosol paint

clear varnish (optional)

If the vase is to be used for cut flowers it is recommended that you paint the inside with one or two layers of clear waterproof varnish to ensure that the paper cut-outs are well-sealed against the water.

1 Carefully cut out the flowers or other images you have chosen from the wrapping paper.

2 Seal with a mixture of 1 part PVA glue to 2 parts water brushed on both sides. Leave to dry.

3 Spread the right side of the flowers generously with wallpaper paste and carefully position on the inside of the pot. Press the back of each flower to remove air bubbles and excess paste. Leave to dry fully. Wipe the inside of the vase with a soft cloth to remove any dried wallpaper paste. Check that each flower is fully stuck down and glue again where necessary. Leave to dry.

A Neo-classical Vase

Use photocopies of classical figures instead of flowers to create a neo-classical vase.

4 Cover the vase with a plastic bag to protect the exterior from the aerosol paint. Make a hole in the bag where it covers the top of the vase and tape it firmly around the neck of the vase.

5 In a well-ventilated room, or preferably outdoors, spray the inside of the vase with the black enamel paint. This is best done with two or three thin layers which are allowed to dry between each coat.

A Vintage Wine Cooler

A galvanized flower bucket has been given a make-over and transformed into an elegant wine cooler to chill white wines and champagne. The bucket was first sprayed a rich shade of cream and then decorated with an eclectic selection of labels saved from favourite wines before being sealed with three coats of clear varnish.

Collect your labels by soaking empty wine bottles overnight in a bowl of water. Use only those which lift off easily – many labels are now glued on with adhesives which prevent the labels peeling away cleanly, so these labels will not work as well. Similarly, labels which are made from foil or have a foil content will not give a smooth finish. Dry the labels between layers of paper towel and then lay them face down on a smooth surface to dry fully.

Tools and Materials

galvanized flower bucket – 30cm (12in) tall

cream spray paint

a selection of wine labels

pva glue

paintbrushes

wallpaper paste

clear satin varnish

1 Spray the exterior of the bucket with cream paint. If possible do this outside, if not then be sure to work in a well-ventilated room.

2 Seal both sides of the labels by painting on a dilute coat made of 1 part PVA glue to 2 parts water. Leave to dry. Don't worry if wrinkles develop, these will disappear when the labels are pasted onto the bucket.

3 Paint the reverse of the labels generously with wallpaper paste and also apply paste to the bucket where the label is to be positioned. Smooth each label into position and use your finger to remove excess paste, but you needn't be too fastidious as the paste will dry clear. Leave to dry fully.

4 Finally seal the wine bucket with 3 coats of clear satin varnish.

A Stamp-collector's Pot

Colourful stamps can be used to create a vivid patchwork design. Mixed packets of stamps can be bought inexpensively from stamp dealers and large newsagencies.

Sunflower Pot

Sunflowers are enduringly popular, and this traced design perfectly captures their simple beauty. Once the traced design has been transferred onto the pot, the painting is child's play – in fact, with a little help from dad, a child could decorate a pot like this for Mothers' Day.

This shape of pot, known as a 'long Tom' is ideal for a sunflower design as there is room for a good length of stem, but you could also adapt this design for a shorter pot by using only the flower and stem and leaving out the painted flower pot.

To keep the design as simple as possible, the template provided shows only one leaf position, but if you want some variation, do as I have done here and alternate upward and downward pointing leaves.

Tools and Materials

terracotta long tom pot 30cm (12in) tall

tracing paper

pencil

carbon paper

masking tape

acrylic paints

fine paintbrushes

clear satin varnish

25mm (1in) paintbrush

1 Trace the sunflower design on page 39 onto tracing paper.

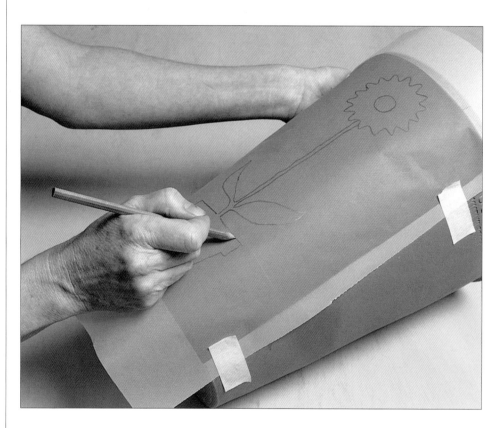

2 Place the carbon paper (carbon side down) onto the pot. Position the tracing over the carbon paper, holding it in place with masking tape, and outline the design in pencil. Remove the tracing and carbon paper to reveal the design. If you wish you can alternate the leaf shapes on adjoining designs for variety.

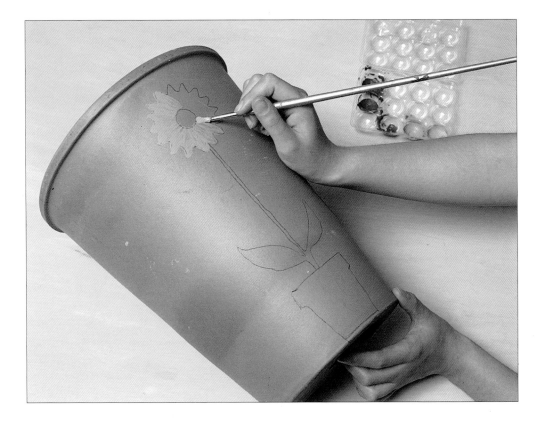

3 Paint the petals yellow and fill in centre with orange paint.

4 Carefully paint the stem and leaves green.

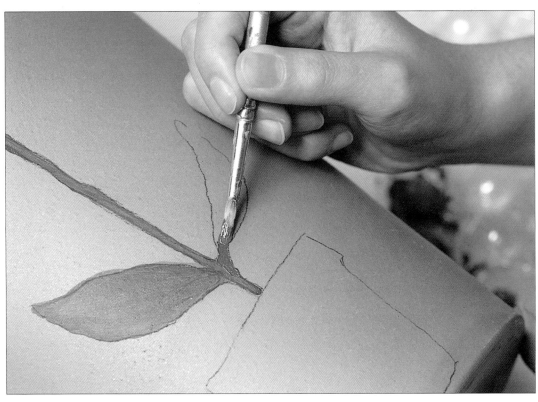

5 Paint the flower pot brown. Don't worry about keeping rigidly to the outlines – variation of line adds to the naive charm of the overall design.

6 To preserve the design, paint the pot with a protective coat of clear satin varnish.

Stencilled Sunflowers

This design can also be used
to cut a sunflower stencil
which can be sponged or
stippled onto a pot. You will
find this works best on hand-
made or weathered terracotta
rather than a new machine-
made pot which won't be quite
absorbent enough for paint
applied in this way.

*Use this template for your
design, or adapt it yourself by
pointing the leaves
downwards or adding more. If
this template does not fit
your pot, reduce or enlarge it
on a photocopier to the
desired size.*

Beaded Pot

Old terracotta pots make excellent containers for all those odds and ends around the home which can look dangerously like clutter unless they are contained in some way or other. Undecorated, the pots have a simple functional elegance, but when embellished with a mesh of silver wire and glass beads they become decorative objects in their own right.

Weathered terracotta pots can be bought cheaply at junk shops, flea markets and car boot sales. Good garden centres often sell them, although they will be more expensive. The glass beads for this project were saved from a broken necklace, but a wide selection of beads is available from haberdashers and craft shops as well as mail order suppliers.

Tools and Materials

**terracotta flower pot –
10cm (4in) diameter**

**reel of fine gauge silver
florist's wire**

scissors

**terracotta-coloured
epoxy putty or self-
hardening clay**

12 glass beads

1 Cut eight 30cm (12in) lengths of silver florist's wire, bundle loosely together and thread 2.5cm (1in) through the hole in the base of the pot.

2 Secure the loose ends with a plug of terracotta-coloured epoxy putty or self-hardening clay.

Bead Lattice

Instead of using beads only where the wires intersect, you can cover all of the wire with beads – large beads where the wires meet and small beads along the length of the wires.

3 Stand the pot upside down on a work-surface and group the wires in pairs. Take each pair of wires over the edge of the pot base, dividing the pot into four equal segments.

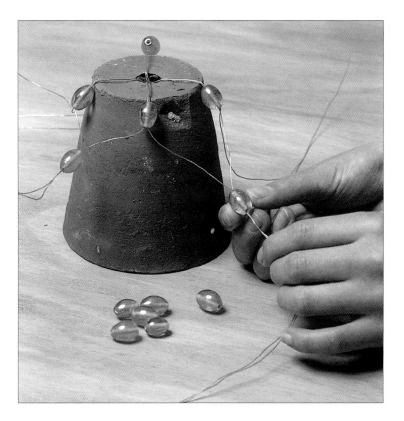

5 Repeat this process adjusting the wire and beads as you work to form an even mesh. Add the final row of beads.

4 Thread each pair of wires through a glass bead. Separate the wires as they emerge from each bead, and join each one to the wire emerging from the adjacent bead. Thread a bead onto the new pair of wires.

6 Bend the wires over the rim of the pot, and hold in position with pieces of epoxy putty or self-hardening clay. Leave to set and trim wire.

Checked Storage Pot

Unless you are a meticulously tidy person it can be difficult to keep the bathroom looking tidy. A selection of terracotta pots of various sizes painted in colours to match your bathroom will look stylish and help solve your storage problems.

Part of the charm of these pots is that they look hand-painted with their irregular strips and the varying thickness of the paint. Don't try to achieve mathematical precision as it is difficult and frustrating to do this by hand and anyway if this is what you want you may as well buy factory-made china. If the idea of painting patterns without any guidelines fills you with horror you can always draw the pattern on the pot in pencil first.

Tools and Materials

small terracotta pots

cream emulsion paint

**powder blue emulsion
    paint**

paintbrushes

small roller

clear satin varnish

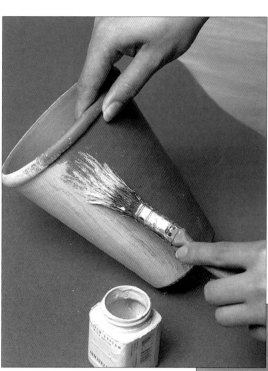

1 Paint the pot inside and out with cream emulsion and leave to dry.

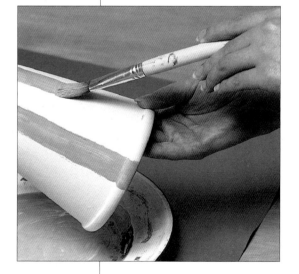

2 Paint blue stripes vertically around the pot.

3 Paint blue stripes horizontally around the pot. Leave to dry.

4 Dilute the paint 50/50 with water and use the roller to apply a pale blue colourwash over the entire surface of the pot.

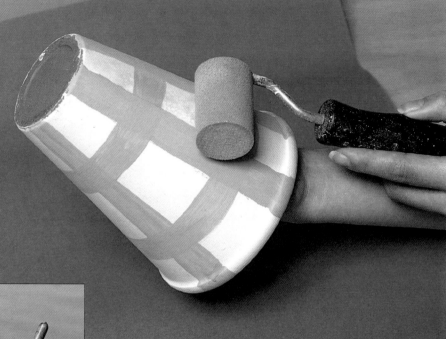

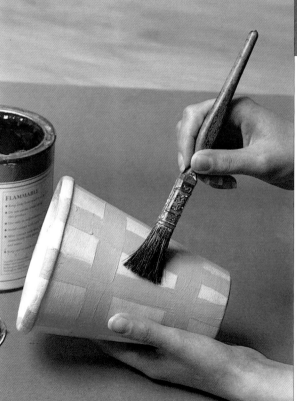

5 Apply a coat of clear satin varnish inside and outside the pot.

Spotted Pot

Create a range of matching pots by using the same colours, but varying the patterns – spots, stripes, diagonals and wavy lines all look effective.

Country Moss and Wire Pot

Plastic flower pots are light and durable but seldom look particularly attractive, so methods of disguising them are always welcome. Here, fine mesh chicken wire and carpet moss have been fashioned into a stylish, easy-to-make cover for a large plastic pot.

Chicken wire is very easy to work with, but it is essential to wear protective gloves as the cut edges can be very sharp. Dried carpet moss can be bought from larger florists and from dried flower suppliers. It should not be gathered from the wild as it is an important food source for woodland creatures. This pot cover is best placed in a shady position as the moss will fade quickly if stood in the full glare of the sun.

Tools and Materials

plastic pot – 30cm (12in) tall

fine mesh chicken wire – 100 x 60cm (3 ⅓ x 2ft)

wire cutters or secateurs

protective gloves

dried carpet moss

1 Cut a wire mesh rectangle 100cm (3 ⅓ft) by 60cm (2ft) and turn in the sharp edges.

2 Lay the carpet moss right side down onto the wire mesh in a central strip 30cm (12in) wide.

3 Place the pot at one end of the moss strip and roll the wire and moss carefully around the pot ensuring that the moss stays in place.

4 Firmly fasten the wire around the pot by interlocking the mesh ends and bending them over one another.

5 Bend the wire over the base of the pot, making firm creases in the wire to ensure a flat base.

Contemporary-style Pot

Instead of using moss between the pot and the wire mesh, paint the pot with a strong coloured matt paint suitable for coating plastic and then cover it with the wire mesh. This would look good in a contemporary setting planted with an architectural plant.

6 At the rim of the pot add extra moss where necessary to ensure that the pot is not visible and fold the wire mesh firmly inside the pot.

Calligraphy Pot

Don't be frightened by the word calligraphy – 'best hand-writing' is probably a more accurate description of the writing on this pot. To make it as easy as possible, pencil guidelines were drawn on the pot and the words were also written in pencil before the marker pen was used.

A selection of botanical names was written around the pot, but if you have a particular herb in mind you could simply repeat the same name a number of times and build up the pattern that way. A horticultural marker pen was used as it is fully waterproof, but you could use a calligraphic felt tip pen instead.

Tools and Materials

terracotta pot – 13cm (5in) diameter

pencil

tape measure

black waterproof marker pen

eraser

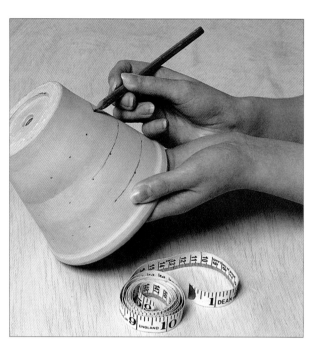

1 Starting from the top of the pot measure and mark four pencilled horizontal bands 2.5cm (1in) apart.

2 Using a pencil carefully write the botanical names on each of the lines.

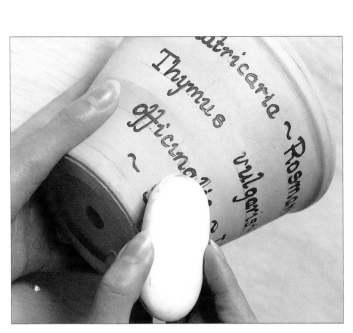

3 Write over the pencilled lettering with the marker pen.

4 Rub out the pencil lines once the ink has dried.

Personalized Pot

Write the Christian names of a friend or a relative around a pot and use it as a container for a gift at Christmas or for a birthday. Use a gold or silver pen for a more festive appearance.

Verdigris Pot

Weathered copper with its beautiful blue-green bloom of verdigris is much sought after, but it is the work of time and cannot be hurried. It is quite easy, however, to decorate a pot with a combination of paints and gilt wax so that it has a passing resemblance to the real thing.

This technique works best on a pot which has a rough texture, as the paints and wax adhere less evenly to the surface, giving a more interesting finish. A verdigris pot looks particularly lovely by candlelight as the gilt finish is highlighted. Use it on the Christmas table or the mantelpiece with ivy and a festive candle.

Tools and Materials

**hand-made long tom –
18cm (7in) tall**

**turquoise emulsion
paint**

cream emulsion paint

paintbrushes

**gilt wax (available from
art shops)**

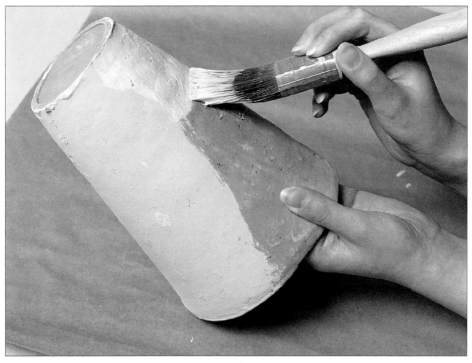

1 Paint the pot with a coat
of turquoise emulsion paint.
Leave to dry.

2 Dip a clean brush into
the cream paint and remove
most of it from the brush by
repeatedly brushing a piece
of paper until the brush is
nearly dry.

3 Lightly brush over the pot with the cream paint – don't
attempt to fully cover the turquoise paint.

4 Use your finger to rub a thin layer of gilt
wax over the pot – the other colours should
still show through.

Painted Glass

It is quite natural to feel nervous when trying a new technique, especially when it involves freehand painting, so if you haven't tried painting on glass before, practise first on a sheet of glass or an old tumbler until you get the feel of the materials.

This type of glass paint is known as contour-lining paste and is usually used to outline areas which are then coloured in with translucent glass paints to create a stained-glass effect, but it can also be used to create a simple raised pattern as has been done for this project. The finished glass can be hand-washed but should not be put in the dishwasher.

Tools and Materials

small glass vase or tumbler approximately 15cm (6in) tall

silver glass contour-lining paste

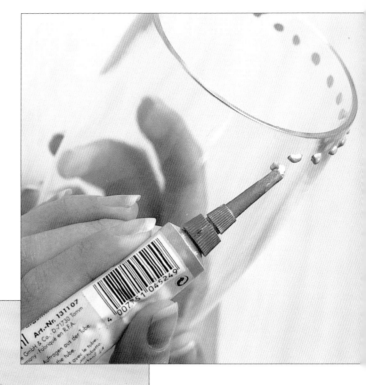

1 Use the contour-lining paste to apply a row of dots close to the rim of the vase. Leave to dry.

2 Apply a second parallel row of dots 4cm (1½in) lower down the vase and leave to dry.

3 Use the paste to draw curly stems between the two rows of dots and again allow to dry.

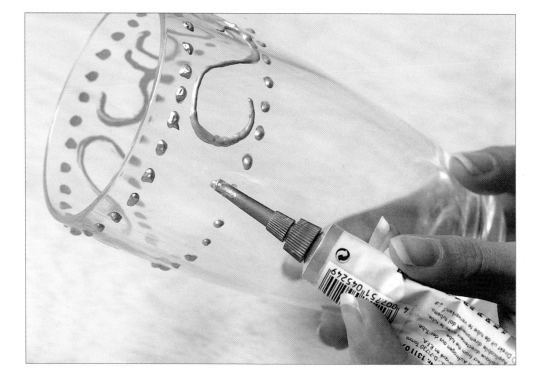

4 Finally add simple flowers consisting of a central dot and radiating petals. Allow to dry.

Stained-glass Effect

Once you have mastered using the contour-lining paste you may wish to experiment with the translucent glass paints and add colour to your designs.

Fresco Pot

Historically, frescoes were painted onto wet plaster which absorbed the paint to give the fresco its characteristic appearance. When new, it was vibrantly colourful, but we are more used to seeing frescoes marked by the ravages of time – faded, fragmented, but still beautiful, and it is this aged beauty which is the inspiration for this project. The techniques are extremely simple and easy. A classically inspired pomegranate design is traced onto the pot and then painted in a pinky-brown colour, slightly darker than the colour of the pot itself. Highlights in dark brown and white are added, before the entire design is gently rubbed back with fine sandpaper to create the effect of centuries of ageing.

Tools and Materials

terracotta pot (if possible made from pale clay) – 15cm (6in) tall

tracing paper

pencil

carbon paper

burnt sienna, burnt umber and white acrylic paint

small artist's paintbrushes

fine sandpaper

clear matt varnish (optional)

1 Trace or photocopy the pomegranate design from pages 70–71. Place the carbon paper, carbon side down, onto the pot, position the tracing in place over the carbon paper and secure with masking tape. Outline the design in pencil and remove the carbon and tracing paper.

2 Use all three paints to mix a pinky-brown colour and paint the entire pomegranate design this colour.

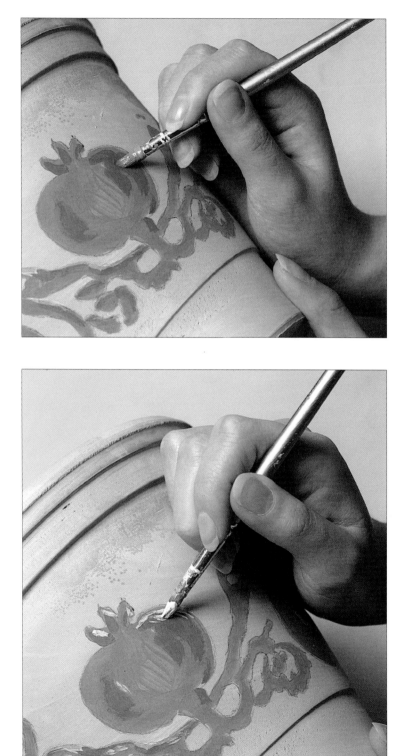

3 Add more burnt umber to the paint and fill in shadows.

4 Add a few white highlights. Allow to dry.

5 Carefully rub back the design with the sandpaper so that it loses its solidity and takes on an aged appearance. To preserve the design you can seal the pot with clear matt varnish (optional).

Top

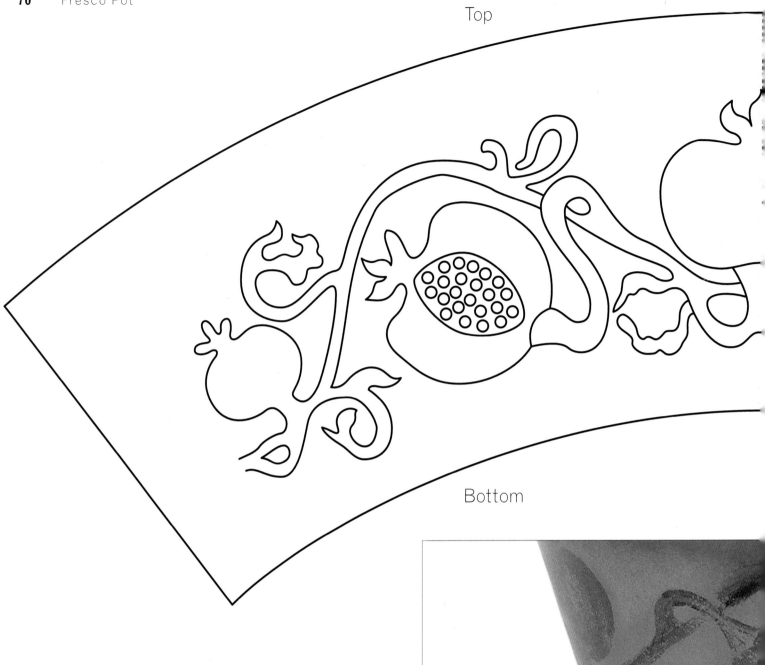

Bottom

Vine Leaf Pot

A design of vine leaves and bunches of grapes would look very authentic when given the 'fresco' treatment.

Trace this template onto tracing paper, carefully butting up the dotted lines to complete the design. If this template does not fit your pot, you can reduce or enlarge the two halves of the design on a photocopier and then join them together.

Mosaic Tile Pot

This pot uses tesserae which are the small glass tiles that are usually used for mosaic designs. They are most commonly sold in square sheets mounted on backing paper, and you can sometimes buy mixed bags of different coloured tiles from your tile merchant.

On a small scale like this there is no need to get involved with tile cement and grouting – these tesserae have simply been stuck in place with PVA glue, and by using a geometric design which does not cover the entire surface of the pot, you will not need to cut any of the tiles.

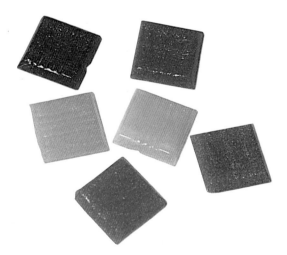

Tools and Materials

rectangular terracotta pot – 22cm (9in) tall and 15cm (6in) wide at rim

a sheet of turquoise blue tesserae

8 royal blue tesserae

pva glue

1 Set the tesserae on the work surface as you intend to position them on the pot.

2 Measure the pattern and the pot to check that the tiles will fit on the pot and adjust the pattern as necessary.

3 Lay the pot on its side, and, starting at the top, glue the tesserae in position.

4 Repeat for all four sides of the pot. Leave to dry.

Mirror-effect Pot

Use mirror tiles instead of the turquoise tesserae for a real art deco effect, especially if the royal blue tesserae are still included in the design.

Tribal Pot

Aboriginal dot paintings of Australian animals are the inspiration for this project. Lizards, snakes, guinea fowl and duck-billed platypuses, painted in earth tones of acrylic paint, scramble and slither around the terracotta pot. This type of dot painting can be quite time-consuming, which is why only the creatures have been given this treatment – in most Aboriginal paintings the surroundings would also consist of dots – but if you enlarge the images somewhat you can use a cotton wool bud instead of a paintbrush and the whole process will become a lot faster, in which case you could fill in the background around the animals.

Tools and Materials

wide-necked terracotta urn – 25cm (10in) tall and 20cm (8in) diameter

tracing paper

pencil

carbon paper

black waterproof marker pen

earth-toned acrylic paints, plus black and white

small artist's paintbrushes

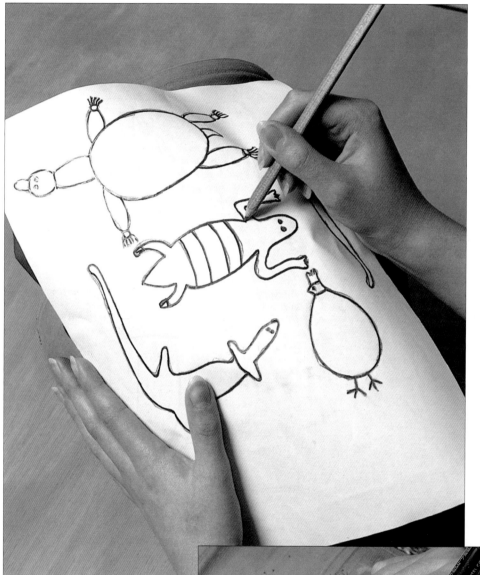

1 Trace the animals from page 80 and use the carbon paper to transfer the images to the pot.

2 Outline each traced image of the animals with the black marker pen.

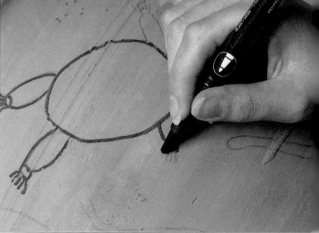

3 Use the same marker pen to divide each animal into segments.

4 Fill each segment with dots of one colour of acrylic paint, until each animal is complete.

Kelim Pot

Copy a traditional pattern from a kelim carpet and use it to decorate a pot, first outlining the image with black marker pen and then painting the design in rich blues and reds.

Trace these templates onto tracing paper and use carbon paper to transfer them to your pot. If you wish, you can use a photocopier to enlarge or reduce the animals.

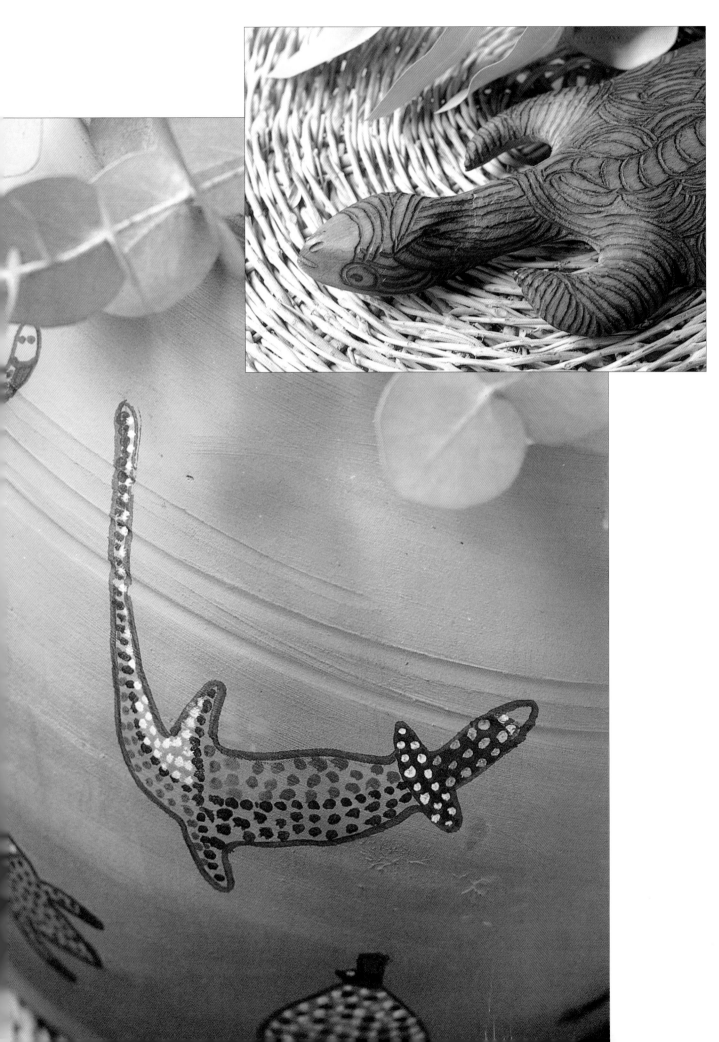

Fern-Patterned Vase

Real etched glass requires considerable skill and a great deal of patience, but there is a far quicker and easier way to create a similar effect with nothing more than an aerosol can of etching spray, spray mount and some pressed leaves. I have used ferns for this vase, but any leaf with a clearly defined outline can be used.

You should have no difficulty finding a suitable vase, these days most high street stores have a selection in their homeware departments – choose one which has straight or sloping sides rather than curves as this will be easier to work with.

Tools and Materials

clear glass vase – 25cm (10in) tall

methylated spirits

pressed leaves or ferns

spray mount

glass etching spray

1 Wash the vase thoroughly, dry and wipe the surface with methylated spirits to ensure good adhesion of the etching spray.

2 In a well-ventilated room spray the top side of the fern leaves with spray mount and carefully position them on the vase, pressing each frond in place.

3 Spray the vase with etching spray, following the manufacturer's instructions for the best results. You will get a better finish if you apply three thin coats rather than one heavy one. Allow 5 minutes drying time between applications.

4 Leave to dry fully for one hour and then peel off the fern leaves. Gently wash off any small pieces of leaf which get left behind. Vases decorated in this way can be hand-washed, but should not be placed in a dishwasher.

Letter-etched Vase

Use rub-down letters instead of fern leaves to write the word 'Flowers' around the rim of the vase. Or why not inscribe the name of your favourite flower as a subtle hint to friends and family?

Bright As A Button

There was a time when every household had a button box – an invaluable resource for mending clothes as well as a treasure chest of riches for small children. Buttons also featured as cheap, easily available decorative accessories for all kinds of projects.

You will need quite a lot of buttons for this project. Junk shops and charity shops are a really good source – house clearances often yield boxes of buttons and they bag them up and sell them very cheaply. Choose matching styles, shapes and colours for your pot or just close your eyes, pour all your buttons into a pile and grab a random handful for a wildly colourful, eclectic look.

Tools and Materials

plastic pot – 25cm (10in)

plenty of old buttons

clear craft glue

tweezers

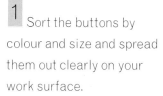

1 Sort the buttons by colour and size and spread them out clearly on your work surface.

2 Select a group of around 20 buttons, so that you have an interesting mix, and glue them onto the pot with about 2cm (1in) between them. Press each one firmly into position and leave each group to set for about 5 minutes before adding further buttons.

4 Any stray threads of glue can be picked off with a pair of tweezers.

3 Repeat this process until the whole of the outside surface of the pot has an even covering of buttons.

Dressing-table Pot

Glue mother-of-pearl shirt buttons onto a small terracotta pot to make elegant storage for a dressing table or bathroom shelf.

A Quick Transformation

A length of rope or string can be used to transform a pot in minutes. Although any shape of pot can be used, this type of decoration looks particularly effective when it is used on an urn-shape. Rope-covered pots make attractive decorative accessories, especially when different-sized pots are grouped together as a still life.

A word of warning – if the rope gets wet, it will shrink as it dries, and if it is tightly coiled around a

terracotta pot it can actually shatter the pot, so this pot should be for indoor use only.

Sisal rope is available from craft shops and DIY outlets.

Tools and Materials

terracotta pot 20cm (8in) tall

clear craft glue

2m (6 ft) sisal rope

1 Apply a line of craft glue just under the rim of the pot.

2 Coil one end of the rope around the pot under the rim, covering the line of glue.

3 Angle the cut end of the rope downwards against the surface of the pot and position the second coil tightly against the first, covering the cut end as you wrap round the second coil.

4 Continue coiling the rope around the pot until you near the base. Apply a second line of glue at the base of the pot to hold the final coil in position.

5 Turn the pot upside down, and apply glue over the whole of the base.

Ethnic Coiled Pot

To give your pot an ethnic look use black sisal instead of natural rope and thread decorative objects onto the string as you coil it into place.

6 Continue coiling the rope on the base of the pot until you reach the centre. Trim the end of the rope.

Classic Silver and Gold Pot

This pot would not look out of place amongst the work of a contemporary silversmith with its delicate tracery of gold leaves on a silver background. In fact, it is a simple terracotta pot which has been transformed in minutes into an object of considerable beauty with two colours of spray paint, spray mount and some pressed leaves.

This is done by first spraying the entire pot gold, then using the spray mount to fasten the leaves to the pot and then applying a coat of silver spray over the pot and the leaves. Once the paint is dry the leaves are peeled away to reveal their golden shadows.

Tools and Materials

terracotta pot – 22cm (9in) tall

gold spray paint

pressed leaves

spray mount

silver spray paint

1 Ensure pot is clean and then spray the surface evenly with gold paint. Leave to dry.

2 Use spray mount to attach the pressed leaves to the surface of the pot in an attractive pattern.

3 Spray the pot and leaves with a coat of silver paint. Leave to dry.

4 Carefully peel away leaves to reveal pattern.

Classic Combinations

Any combination of two colours can be used, depending on the effect you wish to create – red and black look good in an oriental setting, and midnight blue and gold look wonderful amongst heavy velvets and sumptuous brocades.

Transparently Beautiful

Glass looks wonderful by candlelight as the flickering light reflects in the glass. This is particularly true with this small glass vase which has been decorated with a garland of glass buttons threaded onto very fine silver wire. When used as a candle holder it sparkles with light.

Most modern buttons are made from plastic rather than glass, so if you want the real thing you will need to visit your local junk shops and flea markets. Faceted plastic buttons can be used instead, but they don't have the same lustrous quality as glass. If you can't tell the difference, check them by tapping them against your teeth. The difference will be painfully obvious!

Tools and Materials

**square glass vase –
20cm (8in) high**

**glass buttons, clear
and pastel colours**

fine silver wire

**strong, clear adhesive
suitable for glass**

masking tape

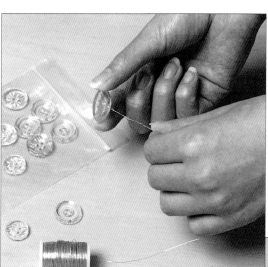

1 Thread wire through the holes of a button going from the back of the button through to the front and back again. Twist the wire behind the button to secure the end of the wire.

2 Glue the button onto the vase and tape firmly in place. Leave to dry.

3 Thread further buttons onto the wire a few at a time.

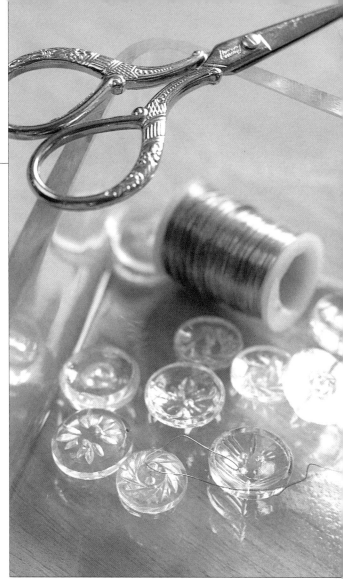

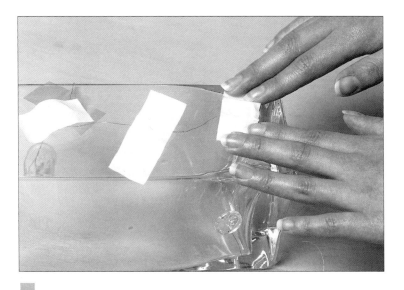

4 Glue the buttons in place on the vase, again using the masking tape to hold them in position. Remove the tape once the glue has dried fully.

5 When you are happy with the number of buttons on the vase, thread on the final button, twist the wire behind it to finish off the end, and glue and tape it in place.

Elegant Night-light Holders

If you have lots of glass buttons, thread them onto wire and use them coiled around jam jars filled with night lights for an evening party in summer. Don't bother gluing them in place, simply hook the wire over the rim of the jar.

Relief Decorated Pot

Epoxy putty or self-hardening clay can be used to create simple and attractive relief decoration on plain terracotta pots for use outdoors or in. Once you have discovered how easy it is to embellish plain pots this way you can become more adventurous with your designs, but start with something simple like this coiled pattern which will give you the feel of the material.

Epoxy putty is available in various colours including terracotta, which is useful not only for decorating pots, but also for repairing them. The white putty can be used to create a contrasting design, or once the decoration is dry the whole pot can be sprayed another colour.

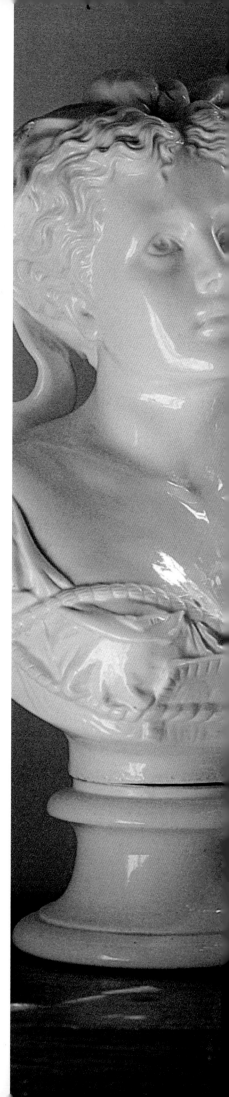

Tools and Materials

terracotta pot – 13cm (5in) diameter

epoxy putty or self-hardening clay

small bowl of water

white spray paint

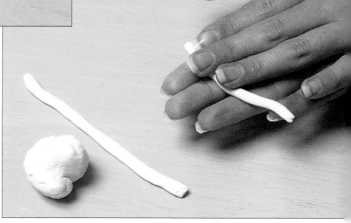

1 Blend the epoxy putty thoroughly, kneading it into a pliable consistency.

2 Roll the epoxy putty between your hands to make a thin, even rope.

3 Dip the rope of epoxy putty into the water.

Greek Border Pot

An old terracotta pot with
plenty of character of its
own does not need to be
covered with a design.
A simple line of decoration just
below the rim is all that's needed.

4 Coil the rope into position on the pot, pressing gently to
ensure good adhesion. Leave to harden overnight.

5 Spray the pot with the
white paint and leave to dry.

Twig and Cone Pot

The decoration on this pot is based on a traditional Bavarian craft which was used to decorate the inside of lodges and summerhouses. Interpreted on a smaller scale, it is used to embellish a large clay pot which becomes a perfect container for a specimen conifer or the family Christmas tree. By dividing the pot into sections with the twigs, different segments are created which are then filled with cones to create a random, but harmonious pattern. Varnishing the finished pot will extend the life of the decoration.

If you don't have a source of twigs, you can use cinnamon sticks which are available from dried flower specialists as are small cones. It is important to use the correct glue sticks to achieve good adhesion – they should be suitable for wood and cellulose.

Tools and Materials

terracotta pot – 30cm (12in) diameter

twigs of various lengths

glue gun and glue sticks

1 kg (23lbs) small cones

secateurs

1 Divide the pot into eight sections by gluing twigs vertically onto the pot. The sections do not need to be the same size – it is more interesting if they vary.

2 Decorate each section with different-sized twigs in various patterns, by gluing the twigs diagonally, or in a diamond or any other pattern which appeals to you.

3 Build the pattern at random, ensuring the twigs and cones butt up quite tightly.

4 Once the twig framework is complete, fill all the gaps with the small cones. If the cones are too tall they can be cut in half with secateurs.

Pebble Pot

Small, smooth stones or shells can be used instead of cones, but be sure to keep them fairly small or the pot will be very heavy. You can use tile cement or a cement mix to fasten them to the pot instead of glue for a more robust adhesion.

Découpage Ocean Scene

For this project, photocopies of fish have been carefully cut out and used with some fairly simple hand-painting to make a vivid, decorative plant pot.

The fish pictures were photocopied onto deep yellow paper – photocopies can be very effective for this sort of work, but if you would prefer more realistic images, look through magazines for photographs of fish which you can colour photocopy.

The terracotta pot was painted with emulsion paint, then the fish were pasted in position and the plants were painted with acrylic paint. With the design complete the pot was sealed with three coats of satin varnish, but you could add more for an even richer finish.

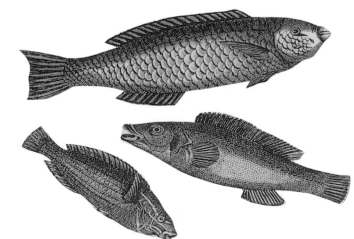

Tools and Materials

terracotta pot – 25cm (10in) diameter

pale green emulsion paint

paintbrushes

photocopied fish images – at least two of each

scissors

pva glue

wallpaper paste

sponge

pencil

acrylic paints

artist's paintbrushes

clear satin varnish

burnt umber acrylic paint

1 Paint the pot with at least two coats of the emulsion paint. Leave to dry.

2 Photocopy the images on page 117, enlarging or reducing to the size you require, then carefully cut out them out.

3 Seal the photocopies with a mixture of 1 part PVA glue to 2 parts water and leave to dry.

4 Paste the fish onto the pot using wallpaper paste applied to the reverse of the fish and to pot. Wipe away excess paste with a sponge. Leave to dry.

5 First sketch the plants and seaweed onto the pot with a pencil and then paint them in with acrylic paints.

6 Seal the pot with at least three coats of satin varnish to which a tiny amount of burnt umber acrylic paint has been added to 'antique' the finish.

Butterfly Pot

Change the setting of your scene from sea to sky. Here, photocopied images of butterflies flutter amongst hand-painted flowers and foliage against a sky blue background.

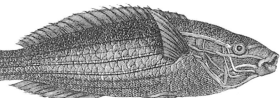

Photocopy these fish onto coloured paper, enlarging or reducing if necessary, to create your ocean scene.

Desk Top Tidy

A small terracotta pot is given the executive treatment. Painted matt black it is lined with scarlet felt and decorated with a tab of red ribbon held in place with gold sealing wax. It would make an ideal Fathers' Day present especially if accompanied by a selection of pens and pencils to replace the motley selection which is usually to be found lurking around the desktop.

Trim the wick of the sealing wax before you light it or you may find that burning wick drops onto the ribbon and sets it alight. In the absence of a family seal for the sealing wax, you can use any small relief decoration such as the handle of a small spoon.

Tools and Materials

terracotta pot – 10cm (4in) diameter

black enamel aerosol paint

tracing paper

pencil

red felt

scissors

10cm (4in) red ribbon 1cm (1in) wide

craft glue

gold sealing wax

teaspoon with decorative handle (optional)

1 Spray the outside of the pot with the enamel paint. Do this outdoors or in a well-ventilated room. Leave to dry.

2 Trace the outline of the pot onto tracing paper and use it to cut four pieces of felt to line the inside of the pot.

3 Cut the end of the ribbon into a 'v' and position so that it hangs half-way down the exterior of the pot. Glue the other end inside the pot.

4 Glue the felt pieces in place inside the pot.

5 Lay the pot on its side, and holding the ribbon in place, drop melted sealing wax onto it to fasten the ribbon to the pot.

6 Press the handle of the spoon into the wax to create an ornamental pattern in the soft wax. Leave to harden.

Furry Pen Pot

For a tactile and modern variation, cover the outside of the pot with fake fur fabric and spray paint the inside with a toning paint.

Blue and White Mosaic Pot

Most of us have a box of broken china tucked away somewhere – often the remains of a favourite set of plates that you always intended to try and repair. In the absence of such a collection, charity shops and junk stalls are a good source of cracked and chipped plates which are sold off very cheaply. Take care when breaking china – place it between several layers of newspaper to prevent fragments flying everywhere, and wear gloves to protect your hands.

The type of pot used for this project is a 'long tom', a tall, narrow pot without a rim. It has a pleasingly architectural shape which is ideal for covering with mosaic. The broken china is interspersed with blue glass stones which help emphasize the colouring of the china and create strong highlights. A pot like this looks wonderful filled with cut flowers or can be planted with blue or white flowering plants.

Tools and Materials

long tom pot – 30cm (12in) tall

a good selection of broken china pieces not more than 2.5cm (1in) square

a tub of white combined tile cement and grout

blue glass stones

sponge

paper towels

scouring pad

1 Lay all the mosaic pieces out on your work surface. You will find it helpful to separate the different patterns so that you can select them easily as you put together your mosaic.

2 Cover approximately one third of the pot with a 1cm (½in) layer of tile cement.

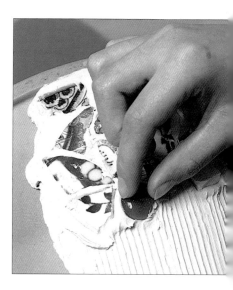

3 Starting at the top of the pot, position the pieces of china in the cement using the different patterns and different size pieces to ensure maximum variety. Add a blue glass stone for every 20 pieces of china.

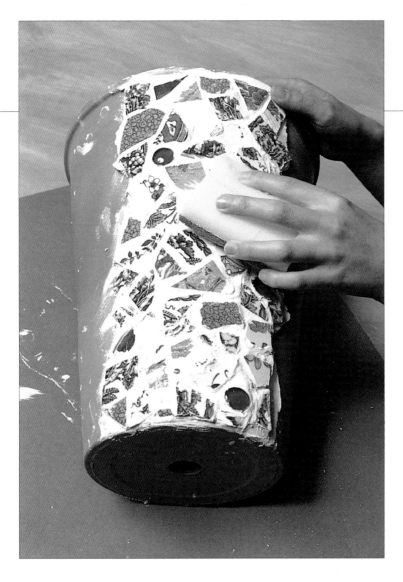

China and Glass Mosaic Pot

Use broad bands of broken china interspersed with a line of glass stones for a less random pattern.

4 When the first panel is complete, wipe over gently with a damp sponge and leave it until the tile cement is firm but not hard. At this stage you can smooth down any uneven surfaces and remove any cement from the surface of the china. Wipe over with a damp sponge and polish with paper towel.

5 Repeat steps 2–4 until the entire pot is covered with mosaic. Fill any gaps between the pieces of china with tile grout. This is most easily done with your fingers, but be careful not to hurt yourself on sharp edges of the china. Wipe over with a damp sponge again and polish with a scouring pad to remove any grout from the surface of the china.

Index

Acknowledgements

I would like to thank my daughter, Charlotte, for allowing me to use her cat sculpture on page 13. Thanks too to Tim Cross for his invaluable help with the fresco design, to Jemma Cox for acting as hand model and also Käthe Deutsch and Martyn Saunders, and Bill Higham and David Reeves for allowing us to use their homes as locations. I am also grateful to Nakota Curios, 12 Courthouse Street, Old Town, Hastings, TN34 3BU (01424 438 900) for the loan of the props on pages 66–67.

Suppliers

Country Gardens Nursery
Bexhill Road, St Leonards on Sea,
East Sussex TN38 8AR
(01424 443 414)
Terracotta pots

The Milliput Co.
Unit 8, The Marian, Dolgellau,
Mid Wales LL40 1UU
01341 422562
Epoxy putty (mail order)

Florist's wire is available from florists and craft shops.

Dried carpet moss is available from dried flower suppliers and large florists.

Glass etching spray is available from art and craft shops.

Small rollers are available from DIY outlets and craft shops.